Writings Notes

A Study Guide to

CHINUA ACHEBE'S

ANTHILLS OF THE SAVANNAH

BY
KUNLE ABRAHAMS

Published 2007 by arima publishing

www.arimapublishing.com

ISBN 978-1-84549-258-8

© Kunle Abrahams 2007

Author Agent:
Goldmark Publishing
23, Ladipo Kuku Street
Box 9698, Ikeja, Lagos.
t: (+234) 01 7933690

Book Pagination - KRIS OSUAGWU
Cover Book Design - ALICIA VIRGINS COMMUNICATION

All rights reserved

This book is copyright. Subject to statutory exception and to provisions of relevant collective licensing agreements, no part of this publication may be reproduced, stored in a retrieval system, or transmitted in any form or by any means, without the prior written permission of the author.

Printed and bound in the United Kingdom

Typeset in Garamond 11/14

This book is sold subject to the conditions that it shall not, by way of trade or otherwise, be lent, re-sold, hired out, or otherwise circulated without the publisher's prior consent in any form of binding or cover other than that which it is published and without a similar condition including this condition being imposed on the subsequent purchaser.

Abramis is an imprint of arima publishing

arima publishing
ASK House, Northgate Avenue
Bury St Edmunds, Suffolk IP32 6BB
t: (+44) 01284 700321

www.arimapublishing.com

Contents

Preface	5
Chinua Achebe's background	6
Chinua Achebe's writing	7
Plot	9
Settings	12
Chapter summaries, critical commentaries & glossaries	14
Chinua Achebe's style and language	38
The characters Sam, Chris, Ikem, Beatrice, Elewa, Emmanuel	41
Themes	49
Writing tips	55
Study questions on *Anthills of the Savannah*	59
Sample answers in note form	60
Further reading	62

Chapter references in these Notes may be used with any edition of *Anthills of the Savannah*.

PREFACE

Writings Notes are a series of newly introduced study guides which the students will find quite useful, as they prepare for their examinations, where the text, _Anthills of the Savannah_, is set as part of the syllabus. It must be emphasized as with all study guides, that students should not use this guide as a substitute for the text. Students are expected to have read the text through and through before using this study guide.

This guide would among other functions help and encourage students to have an appreciation and informed personal response to literature and general understanding of African literature with all its nuances.

The author of this note is Abrahams Kunle. He has postgraduate qualifications in English and Literary Studies and has taught in tertiary institutions all over Africa.

CHINUA ACHEBE'S BACKGROUND

Albert Chinualumogu Achebe was born in Ogidi, Nigeria on November 16, 1930, the son of Protestant converts, Isaiah Okafo and Janet N. Iloegbunam Achebe. He attended Government College in Umuahia from 1944 to 1947, and the University College, from 1948 to 1953. At the University College Ibadan, then affiliated to the University of London, Achebe studied English, History and Theology.

Achebe joined the NBC in 1954 and by 1961, he had created and founded the Voice of Nigeria (becoming the Director of External Broadcasting) which he ran until the exodus of 1966. He left the NBC to become Senior Research Fellow and later Professor of English at the University of Nigeria, Nsukka. In 1985, he became Emeritus Professor.

He has also been Visiting Professor of English at the University of Massachusetts, Amherst and the University of Connecticut, Storrs, both in USA.

Achebe has published several novels, short stories, essays and children's books among which are his bestsellers, *Things Fall Apart*, and other well-known works like *No Longer at Ease*, *Arrow of God*, *A Man of the People*, *Girls At War*, *Beware Soul Brother*, *Morning Yet on Creation Day* and *The Trouble with Nigeria*.

His volume of poetry was joint-winner of the first ever Commonwealth Poetry Prize. He has received numerous honorary doctorate degrees from universities in the UK, U.S.A, Canada and Nigeria. Amongst his other laurels are the award of a Fellowship of the Modern Languages Association of America, the Scottish Arts Council's Neil Gunn Fellowship, of which he was second recipient, and the Nigerian National Merit Award. In June 2007, Achebe was awarded the prestigious, The Man Booker Prize award for fiction.

CHINUA ACHEBE'S WRITING

Achebe's work is primarily interested in African politics, the depiction of Africa and Africans in the West, and the intricacies of pre-colonial African culture and civilization, as well as the effects of colonialization on African societies. Achebe's 1958 magnum opus *Things Fall Apart*, a historical novel that considers the effects of colonialization on Igbo society, has been translated into over 50 languages. It sets the tone for most of the prose that would emanate from Africa. It is a work that focuses on the colonial era, while mostly highlighting the clash between two cultures; European and African.

Other African works focus on even the pre-colonial era of slavery. Ayi Kwei Armah's *Two Thousand Seasons* (1973), a historical novel set in pre-colonial Africa deals with migrations of peoples, enslavement of Africans by both Arabs and Europeans, and the possibility of resistance to colonialism. Other works by African writers dwell on the eve of African independence taking a peep into what the future has in store when independence is finally achieved. This is the attention of Ngugi Wa Thiong'o's *Petals of Blood*. The final stage of works by African writers to portray the reality of African experience is the situation after Africans have achieved independence. The colonialists have been defeated through warfare as in the case of Mau-Mau in Kenya or through peaceful diplomatic and constitutional manoeuvring. The portrayal of Africa is such that nothing has actually changed. The oppressive colonialists have simply been replaced by the local stooges; the politicians and the military dictators. They have embraced neo-colonialism and have relegated the needs of the masses that fought for the independence to the background. This is the frustration a writer like Ayi Kwei Armah tries to depict in *The Beautiful Ones Are Not Yet Born*.

A founding Editor of *Okike*, a literary magazine, Achebe was also active in the Igbo-language journal of poetry and literary criticism *Uwa ndi Igbo*, as well as numerous other publications. The founding Editor of Heinemann Publisher's African Writers Series, a body of work that has emerged as a cornerstone of postcolonial literature, Achebe was instrumental in introducing the world to new writing from Africa.

His treatise of literary criticism, *An Image of Africa: Racism in Conrad's "Heart of Darkness"* has become one of the most influential, controversial, widely studied and debated essays of its kind in classrooms around the world. Decrying Joseph Conrad as *"a thoroughgoing racist"*, Achebe asserts that Conrad's famous novel dehumanizes Africans, rendering Africa as *"a metaphysical battlefield devoid of all recognizable humanity, into which the wandering European enters at his peril."*

Anthills of the Savannah opens a new epoch in the literary career of Achebe in its departure from his earlier works. The characters in the novel are enlightened and sophisticated city elites. Even for those not so educated, they are not lacking in intellectual maturity. The language in the novel also takes a new verve of intellectual discourse, which could at times evolve through poetic expression. The setting equally has a modern African state in perspective (possibly Nigeria).Modern issues such as gender inequality, good governance, human rights, accommodation of modern practice in a predominantly African setting are treated.

Achebe's novel effort in this work buttresses one of the themes in all his works; the coexistence and interdependence of African and European culture. He explores the world of folktales, African proverbs and other local contents in unity with modern context. This collaboration between two worlds has become inevitable in this fast-paced world of the twenty first century.

PLOT

The story opens with a cabinet meeting of the military regime under Sam. The issue is whether the Head of State would visit the drought-ravaged Abazon, which has become a fortress of opposition to his régime. Insight is given into the subservient and hero-worship attitude of some of the commissioners to the military Head of State. The Information Commissioner called Chris, however, seems to be independent-minded.

The people of Abazon finally decide to pay a courtesy visit to the Head of State, who welcomes it with disdain and apprehension. Later Ikem, a native of Abazon, and a close friend of Chris and the Editor of the government newspaper, *National Gazette*, decides to do a press coverage of the visit, not without an altercation with his boss cum friend, Chris. Other characters like Elewa the girlfriend of Ikem, Beatrice the girlfriend of Chris and Mad Medico are introduced.

One turning point in the novel is the meeting of Ikem and the elders of Abazon. Before this time, Ikem and even Chris have been under the suspicion of the military government for their criticisms and intellectual independence.

At the reception, Ikem is well received by the elders of the Abazon. From the speech of the chief spokesman, it is obvious that the people of Abazon look up to Ikem for direction in whether to support the military regime or not. After the meeting, Ikem is accosted by a police officer for a flimsy traffic offence, as an excuse for having attended the meeting with the elders of Abazon.

Sam orders Chris to issue a suspension letter to Ikem who refuses on the grounds that there is no tangible evidence that Ikem has been instigating the people of Abazon against the government. When Chris would not budge, Sam uses all kinds of subtle threat and intimidation to coerce Chris to issue the letter. Chris decides to resign his own appointment from Sam's cabinet, but Sam refuses, issuing more threats, but he however manages to make a fictitious Chairman, Board of Directors of Kangan Newspapers Corporation, publishers of *National Gazette* to issue the suspension letter to Ikem.

Having been sacked, Ikem now seems to have more freedom to express his views against the government. When the invitation comes for him to give a talk in the University of Bassa, he uses it as fulcrum to express his philosophies and principles concerning the military government. One of his clarifications is on the issue of *"democratic dictatorship of the proletariat"* which the people have ignorantly embraced as an alternative to military dictatorship and whose desirability he disagrees with. Rather he calls for a sense of responsibility such that every citizen does not heap any blame on neo-colonialism. Self-purge and accountable leadership according to him are the ingredients for good leadership.

However in the course of the talk, a student asks his opinion on the rumour concerning the president's intention of putting his bust on a currency. Ikem innocently answers *"...any serving president foolish enough to lay his head on a coin should know he is inciting people to take it off; the head I mean"*. This simple statement is later misrepresented and sensationalized in the *National Gazette* as "EX-EDITOR ADVOCATES REGICIDE".

From this point, the government begins its onslaught on opposition. Mad Medico is summarily repatriated to his home country, England. Major Johnson Ossai, the hatchet man of Sam is promoted. Ikem suddenly disappears and his search begins. Chris and Beatrice later find out that some men in uniform have abducted Ikem. The government further continues its propaganda by labelling Ikem a coup plotter who is attempting to destabilize the government. The government announcements continue and in its final offensive announces that in the process of arresting Ikem, a scuffle results during which Ikem sustains a fatal injury.

Somebody with the understanding of Chris knows that the information given by the government concerning Ikem simply means that Ikem has been murdered, so he knows that his own life is in danger. He begins hiding to escape the onslaught of the repressive government. Ikem joined by Emmanuel the President of the Student Union of the University of Bassa and the taxi driver, Braimoh, all begin moving from one hide out to another.

Chris and his group finally begin their journey to the Great North Road, in Abazon. For Chris, this journey is symbolic for two reasons. It is the home of slain Ikem and the stronghold of opposition to the military regime.

On their journey, they run into a mob in jubilation and rowdy merriment. On investigation, they are told that the military government has been overthrown. In the euphoria of the recent development, they all decide to return to Bassa, but something bizarre is about to happen. A police officer is on the verge of raping a girl called Adamma and nobody is interested. In his conscientious zeal, Chris confronts the man and in the process, Chris is shot dead.

Beatrice takes the death of her fiancé stoically, especially when there is a new life that needs her attention. (Elewa the girlfriend of Ikem is pregnant).Beatrice also derives some solace from her new friends – Captain Abdul Medani, Adamma, Emmanuel, Elewa and Agatha.

Elewa finally gives birth to a baby girl. When there is the possibility of the mother and uncle of Elewa not being present to perform the naming ceremony, due to some cultural reservations, Beatrice performs the ceremony. She gives the child the name-Amaechina (May -the –path- never -close) literally meaning, *there should be continuity in my lineage* .When the mother and uncle of Elewa finally arrive the scene of the ceremony, the uncle supports the decision of Beatrice in naming the child, instead of waiting for custom to hold sway.

Emmanuel who happens to be at the scene of Chris' death gives Beatrice the last words of her fiancé as *"The Last Grin".* Beatrice understands that what Chris is trying to say is *"the last green bottle"* .To her, this statement is like the missing key. She compares the contentment in death experienced by Chris to the agony of death experienced by her father. This alone gives her the satisfaction that her friend, Chris did not die in vain, as he died mocking death itself.

SETTINGS

The author tactically downplays any easily recognized location. One obvious fact however is that the novel is set in Africa. Kangan is the country of the novel and the microcosm of African continent. Some critics have placed Kangan in the ambiance of Nigeria. Bassa is the capital city and the seat of power, while Abazon the stronghold of opposition to the military regime is situated in the remote far North.

Achebe presents an African country which has gained its independence from a European country and has experienced democratic rule, but which at the moment is under the hegemony of an oppressive military government. This setting is apposite and appropriate because it depicts activities that are applicable in most African countries.

Bassa is the seat of power and where most of the actions in the novel take place .It is situated in the southern part of the country and it seems to have arrogated all development to itself. It boasts of all government machinery such as the *National Gazette,* the mouthpiece of the government, the Government Residential Area (GRAs), and even the President Guest House in a suburb called Abichi.

Abazon is located in the far north. The citizens of this province are at the forefront of opposition to the military regime. Ikem is notably from this area. When the elders of Abazon visit the Head of State in solidarity, the government in its confrontational mien perceives it as an invasion. Chris, towards the end of the story, has to escape to Abazon and gives the following reasons:

> *The choice of Abazon as sanctuary came quite naturally. At the purely sentimental level it was Ikem's native province which although he had rarely spent much time there in recent years...then it was a province of unspecified and generalized disaffection to the regime. One could indeed call it natural guerilla country ...*

In terms of infrastructural development, Abazon as a province has suffered untold neglect by the military government deliberately to pummel it into submission, for its opposition to the military regime. Chris comments on this during his flight to Abazon, *"Even the asphalt on which* **Luxurious** *sped towards the North told its own story of two countries".*

Ironically for Chris, Abazon is where he runs to for succour and where he accidentally meets his death in the hands of a trigger-happy police officer. He dies in a settlement not far from Agbata in Abazon. The novel however ends in Bassa where it begins. This structural device is to bring about a unity between the formerly estranged Bassa and Abazon. The seed of Ikem in the new baby (Amaechina-May the Path Never Close) returns to Bassa and from his name, to continue from where his father stops the struggle.

The setting of the story is complemented by its cultural content in language, norms and characterization.

CHAPTER SUMMARIES, CRITICAL COMMENTARIES & GLOSSARIES

Chapter 1

The story opens on a dramatic note at a cabinet meeting between the President and his commissioners. The discourse is the President's visit to Abazon, the drought-ravaged province and the fortress of opposition to his government. Chris, the Information Commissioner, advises the President to visit the area.

The chapter gives an insight into some of the members of the cabinet, most of who are portrayed as sycophants and ever ready to pander to all the whims of the president. Chris however appears to be the only person with the guts to openly express his opinion without any pretence. There are many reasons for this. He used to be a classmate of the President and he actually recommends most of the cabinet members. More so, Chris is also an intellectual libertine. Professor Okong is a contrast to Chris. He thrives on banality and possesses questionable academic credentials. Sam, the Head of State is at the centre of all adulation. He used to be a naïve military man before he learns the ropes and he now sees himself as infallible and his opinion never to be contradicted.

Commentary

The military tone of the opening sentence sets the atmosphere that would pervade the novel: *"You 're wasting everybody's time, Mr. Commissioner for Information. I will not go to Abazon. Finish! Kabisa! Any other business?"*

Chris' objection to the view of the Head of State also gives an insight into his independence. The array of commissioners that would pander to all the caprices of the President depicts a picture of a nation under siege, where the leader is autocratic and no voice of dissent is tolerated. Sam caricatures a typical African monarch whose word is law.

The impending visit of the people of Abazon shows the line of opposition the military regime would have to contend with in the course of the story. The Abazonians represent the popular voice of the masses. The apposite imagery of the people of Abazon as a *"storm"* is symbolic. Despite all the air of invincibility that surrounds the President, he expresses his reservation in meeting the *"storm".*

CHAPTER SUMMARIES, CRITICAL COMMENTARIES & GLOSSARIES

GLOSSARY
Kabisa-*A military jargon meaning that is the end of the matter.*
Propitious auguries-*invocation or appeasement*
Rainmakers-*Those who can use some magical means to either cause rain to fall, stop it from falling, or divert it to fall elsewhere.*
Danshiki-*A loose gown often worn by men in West Africa*
Guinness Book of Records-*An annual publication that chronicles feats and achievements of mankind in all areas of human endeavour*
Sandhurst-*A British military school known for training officers in Britain, but which has also trained military officers from the Commonwealth of nations.*

Chapter 2
More insight is given into the psyche of the President as he views the solidarity visit of the Abazon elders as tantamount to an invasion. Professor Okong is sent by the President to *"gauge the temperature"* of the visitors and calm them down. He is also to lie that the President is busy on a phone call to the President of the United States of America. In the President's interaction with Professor Okong and the Attorney General, it is obvious that they could do anything to please and flatter the President, even going to the extent of using bad language against their other colleagues just to curry the favour of the President.

Commentary
This chapter further explores the psychology of a dictator who lives with the phobia of being invaded just as he has invaded the state to impose his illegitimate rule. The neo-colonial mentality of a typical African leader is shown when he prides himself as speaking to the President of the United States of America, instead of attending to the domestic needs of the people he is supposed to rule over. Sam would rather isolate himself than interact with the people. The duplicity of the President is apparent in the instruction he gives concerning the media coverage of the visit of the people of Abazon. According to him *"I want you to look at the man you are shaking hands with"* so that the people would be portrayed as being in solidarity with the government. The duplicity at the top rears its ugly head even among the President's subordinates. The commissioners engage in backbiting to discredit their colleagues in a bid to be in the good book of the President. Ironically, instead of appreciating the supposed information leaked concerning their colleagues, the President could see

through them and his opinion of them as being pawns is consolidated. He mocks Professor Okong thus, "Soft to the core. That's what they all are. Professors". There is ambiguity here as to the personality of the President whether he could not stand the fawning attitude of a sycophant or he simply abhors intellectualism.

GLOSSARY
Entebbe Raid-*June 28, 1976 raid by the Israeli commandos to free the Israeli citizens held hostage by Arab terrorists cum hijackers.*
General Big Mouth-*A talkative*
In statu puppillari-*A class of postgraduate students that are a little below the Master's Degree level.*
The Exorcist- *A box office hit motion picture about a young woman who is possessed by a demon, based on a book by William Peter Blatty*
Espirit de corps -*Feeling or spirit of camaraderie among a group.*
Carry their nonsense come your house-*Do not bother me with your frivolities.*
President Ngongo's advice-*A pseudonym for African dictators*

Chapter 3
Chris, in his capacity as the Commissioner for Information, instructs Ikem as the editor of the *National Gazette "to send a photographer to the Reception Room of the Presidential Palace to cover a goodwill delegation from Abazon"*.This issue marks the genesis of conflict between the two friends. While Chris wants to satisfy his master in his capacity as the commissioner, Ikem still sees himself as a literary artist of the libertine ilk and feels that he owes his loyalty to the people of Kangan.

Reluctantly, Ikem begins a journey to the Presidential Palace to cover the visit of the Abazon elders. On his trip, he reminisces on one of his writings entitled, *"Hymn to the Sun"*. He also ruminates on his traffic adventure-a taxi driver that wants to out-manoeuvre him off the road. This scene depicts the aggressiveness of drivers in a typical city in Africa. He continues with his meditation on the omnipotence of the sun, which he narrates in a folklore pattern.

Commentary
This chapter brings to question the role of the press in a developing country. Should the loyalty of the press be to the government in power

which is the main financier and possibly owner of the press or to the generality of the people? Chris in his capacity as a government official finds himself in a dilemma of either following the dictate of his *"employer"* for him to keep his job or follow the radical view of his friend, Ikem, who believes in the objectivity and freedom of the press.

Ikem's meditation entitled, *Hymn to the Sun* captures an essence of the novel. The sun is described as the, *Undying Eye of God* .Coincidentally, the period in the novel coincides with when the sun is at its most ferocious state, when the people have been *"slowly steamed into well-done mutton since February"* .The harshness of this weather symbolically captures all the attributes of the dictatorial Head of State. His omniscience and omnipotence are to be appeased if the people are to have some respite. The author's use of folklore to narrate the *Hymn to the Sun* further confirms his dexterity in capturing a contemporary subject in a traditional ambiance.

GLOSSARY
Sun of April-*A time of the year in the tropics when the weather is unbearably hot.*
National Anthem-*Reference to the Nigerian anthem,* **Arise O Compatriot'**
May Day Celebrations- *A day of the year set aside for workers.*
Mama John-*John's mother.*
Volvo- *A brand of a luxury car*

Chapter 4
Ikem has a quarrel with his uneducated girl-friend, Elewa, as he, Ikem, is about to send her away in a taxi, but she is not happy about what she considers a demeaning attitude to her femininity. *"To put a girl for taxi at midnight to go and jam with arm robbers in the road"*. A taxi comes later and Ikem puts her in it to be conveyed to her house although not without more protestations from her.

After, Ikem begins to ruminate on his attitude towards women generally. He appears to enjoy the sexual satisfaction that Elewa gives him, but not the responsibility that comes with it. Ikem confesses, "*I must get to work. That's the other thing about sleeping together. It prevents work".*

Ikem's mind shifts to the issue of capital punishment as it relates to how he uses his editorials to correct some ills in the society. He ruminates further on his experience at a firing squad incident where some convicted armed robbers are shot. He thinks of the sadistic tendency in the crowd that gather not minding the scorching sun. In the sober mood that is supposed to characterize such event, ironically some pickpockets are busy stealing from the crowd. Even the robbers at stake are not spared the oddity that characterizes the event. One of the robbers prophetically says, "*I shall be born again*". After this experience, Ikem writes an editorial condemning what he considers, "*outrageous and revolting performance*" of shooting convicted armed robbers at stake. Strangely too, the President abrogates shooting convicted armed robbers by tying them to the stake.

Ikem thinks of his last confrontation with Chris, who in his capacity as the Commissioner for Information would like to vet all editorials by Ikem, a practice which he detests. He abhors what he considers government interference in the running of the press. Chris too is in a dilemma of serving a dictator and remaining true to his conscience.

A strange side of the President who appears to admire other notorious African dictators is shown. Sam appears to be still bound in neo-colonialism and the aristocratic style of the English Upper Class.

Commentary

Elewa is the first female character introduced in the novel. She is not educated, yet she is able to strike a deep friendship and passion with a man from a different tribe and social class as Ikem. Her awareness of her right and awareness as a woman is shown in her disdain at being put in a taxi and taken away after Ikem had had carnal knowledge of her. She feels used and would rather Ikem appreciate her beyond this mundane level. She desires more quality time with Ikem. Though an illiterate, she is able to assert her right and possibly teach Ikem some lessons on relationship with the women folk.

Ikem as a journalist gives more insight into some social contradictions in Kangan. He contemplates a system, which publicly executes its victims (the armed robbers).The impunity with which the robbers treat their execution and the audacity of some pick-pockets to still steal reveal the ineffectiveness of capital punishment. The sardonic statement of one of the robbers, "*I shall be born again*", is prophetic of more robbers that would be bred by a social system riddled with many contradictions. The issue of press freedom and the dictatorship of the President are among many of such contradictions.

The chapter ends on a psychological analysis of the President whose only pedantic gain in an OAU meeting is his admiration of "*the old emperor who never smiled nor changed his expression no matter what was going on around him".*

GLOSSARY

Ok Oga-*It is okay, big boss.*
...the Gauls-*an ancient region of Western Europe that included large portions of France, Belgium, and neighbouring parts of Italy, the Netherlands and Germany. It was invaded and conquered by the Romans before 100 BC and again in the Gallic Wars of 58-51 BC under Julius Caesar.*
Senghor- *Leopold Sedar Senghor (1906-2001), president of Senegal (1960-1981), and an internationally respected poet, philosopher, and theoretician. A French-speaking African intellectual, Senghor defended and promoted the cultural heritage of Africans, developing the idea of negritude.*
Mandingauls-*an adulteration of Mandingoes and Gaul (Charles de Gaulle)*
Black Maria-*A huge truck often used to convey convicts and the accused.*
I shall be born again-*A reference to the biblical teaching of turning a new leaf character-wise.*
Public Execution Amendment Decree-*A military law that prohibits public execution of criminals.*
Big Shot-An influential person.
Mozart's Eine Kleine Nachtmusik- *Mozart's composition entitled*, **A Little Night Music**
OAU-*Organization of African Unity now known as African Union. (AU)*
President Ngongo-*A pseudonym for a typical African President.*

Chapter 5

A new character called Mad Medico (MM) whose real name is John Kent is introduced. He is a Briton, but currently employed as a Hospital Administrator in Kangan. His friendship with the like of the President, Ikem and Chris must have attracted him to the country. He is a libertine, a freethinker and aptly described as an *"aborted poet".* The point of attraction must have been the dynamism of the four friends' intellectual discourse as it pertains to dictatorship and governance.

Mad Medico's radicalism is exemplified in the number of controversies he has been embroiled in which must have led to his deportation, if not for the timely intervention of his influential friends. In one of his encounters with controversy, he supports a patient to sue a medical doctor who has conducted himself unethically. In retaliation, a body of doctors instigates his deportation on flimsy grounds.

In this chapter, Mad Medico and his visiting friend, Dick, Ikem, Elewa, Beatrice and Chris are involved in the discussion of different topics ranging from women rights, dictatorship and intellectualism.

Commentary

This chapter marks the only place in the novel where all the critics and oppositionists of the military government meet minds. Mad Medico's sarcasms which earn him a threat of deportation is actually directed at the government and not the sensibility of the Blackman as the doctors are wont people to believe. The use of Sodom and Gonorrhea is an indictment of the decadence in Kangan. Other characters too like Ikem, Dick and Beatrice join in this tirade of sarcasm.

More understanding is also given into the personality of Ikem who does not have much respect for womenfolk. He does not see any need for communication with his girl-friends because of his prejudice that women do not have brains.

Beatrice tries to unravel the cause of altercation between Chris and Ikem. Chris' simplistic explanation that Ikem is envious of him having been his classmate when they were in school, shows Chris' parochial assessment of issues.

This scene is a melting pot of sorts, where characters from different backgrounds, races, professions engage in intellectual assessment of issues of human concerns which are universal.

GLOSSARY
Gordon's Dry Gin-*An English alcoholic drink*
Wahalla-*Hassles*
Blessed are the poor in heart...- *See Matthew 5 in the Bible.*
...Sodom and Gonorrhea-*Adulteration or corruption of the biblical city of Sodom and Gomorrah*
Alka Seltzer-*A character in the novel,* Him She Loves
Petit Bourgeois- *The emerging local upper class or ruling elite.*
ADC-*aide -de –camp/A personal assistant to a high-ranking military officer.*

Chapter 6

Beatrice the fiancée of Chris has been invited by the President to a small private dinner. Different ideas race through her mind on the motive of the invitation. She calls Chris who gives her the encouragement to accept the invitation and to *"stay cool no matter what"*.

As she is being driven to the dinner, Beatrice contemplates the philosophy behind the Presidential Retreat, which she considers as one of the alienation measures of leaders from those they govern. *"Retreat from what? From whom…From the people and their basic needs of water which is free from Guinea worm, of simple shelter and food"*.

At the dinner, Beatrice discovers the motive for her invitation. She discovers that she is merely showcased as an epitome of womanhood in Kangan and to *"arrange to give woman angle"* to the foreign visitors. Ridiculously, she is also to keep an American invited guest company during the dinner.

Commentary

The invitation of Beatrice gives another perspective to the character of the President. Without the knowledge of Chris, he invites his fiancée. This could be a way of the President trying to reach Chris who is fast becoming aloof to his dictatorial ambitions.

Beatrice's maturity in comporting himself at the dinner, has a semblance to the diplomacy of Chris. In contrast, Ikem's tactlessness is obvious. The invitation of Beatrice also shows the attitude of most men to women in an African society. The womenfolk are seen as objects of exhibition just as Beatrice has been invited to showcase Kangan femininity. The portrayal of the scenario as a practice of polygamy adds a comic dimension to the story. *"Then came the master's voice summoning me to have my turn in the bedchamber of polygamy"*. While this should not be read as an outright condemnation of polygamy, it gives a picture of the deception, unfaithfulness and lasciviousness of the ruling class as exemplified through Sam.

Beatrice disparages her role in the whole exercise as she feels she is being used as an object of manipulation, which she is an affront to her femininity, just as Elewa has felt when Ikem decides to forcefully take her home in a taxi.

GLOSSARY
Taj Mahal-*A white marble mausoleum in Agra, Northern India.*

Mazrui-Kenyan *Political Scientist, a professor, well-known for his documentaries on the glorious past of Africa.*

Nkrumah-*Kwame Nkrumah (1909-1972), first prime minister (1957-1960) and president (1960-1966) of Ghana and the first black African postcolonial leader. He was a powerful voice for African nationalism,*

Stalinist Czar-*Joseph Stalin(1879-1953) dictatorial ruler Soviet Union from 1929 until his death.*

Jollof-*A delicacy prepared from rice*

Black is beautiful-*Slogan of the Black Panther Movement, used especially by Stokely Carmichael.*

Moselle-*a light typically dry white wine from West Central Germany*

Quid pro quo-*the giving of something in return for something else, often in a spirit of cooperation*

Castro-*Fidel Castro, the communist leader of Cuba.*

Desdemona Complex-*The wife of Othello who becomes the object of jealousy in the play,* **Othello**

Esther-*A Bible character who used her feminine qualities to liberate her people, the Israelites*

Chapter 7

She contemplates the religious fanaticism of her housemaid, Agatha. From here, she does a reminiscence of her childhood in view of the role of women in an African society where any woman who possesses a little amount of power or influence is said to have used, *"bottom power"* or rather used her sexual attraction to sleep her way to the top. She sees this as nothing short of envy from the men folk who often see women as a threat.

She traces her orientation as an emancipated woman to her background, where as the fifth girl-child, she is never wanted. Her father wants a male child desperately and for her, she feels unwanted. No wonder, she is given the consolatory name *"Nwanybuife"* (A female is also something).This vividly shows a typical African attitude to a female child.

Ikem later visits Beatrice and their discussion of women rights continues. In a confession, Ikem accepts that women have not been fully integrated into the affairs of a male-dominated world. Women according to him are placed on a revered pedestal of isolation from human affairs and are only invited to do damage control.

Commentary

This chapter continues on the same note as the previous one as it dwells on the place of women in a modern society. The envy of the men for a rising woman is alluded to by Beatrice. The attitude of a male-dominated society to an independent woman is also highlighted. The theory of Ikem on the myth of woman degeneration drawing illustration from all human institutions and norms is an eye-opener to the amount of subjection that women have gone through over the years. The paradoxical insight of Ikem is that:

> *So the idea came to man to turn his spouse into the very Mother of God to pick her up and carry her reverently to a nice, corner pedestal up there, her feet completely off the ground she will be just as irrelevant to the practical decisions of running the world as she was in her bad days.*

Ikem equally tries to yoke the oppression suffered by the women-folk to that of the generality of the people. He appears to speak the mind of Achebe himself as it relates to revolution and its imperativeness in changing a society. He expresses the futility of *"sweeping, majestic visions of people rising victorious like a tidal wave against their oppressors and transforming their world with theories and slogans into a new haven and a new earth of brotherhood"*. Beatrice does not just object to an approach, but proffers a solution, *"Reform may be a dirty word then, but it begins to look more and more like the most promising route to success in the real world"*. This confession is a dramatic irony of the approach of all the oppositions in the novel and in the world at large.

GLOSSARY

Gari-A *staple food made from cassava flour*
Madam Pompadour-*Influential mistress of Louis XV, king of France, known for her patronage of art and literature.*
Uwa-t'uwa-*World without end*
Das right-*That is right*
Nwanyi- *Woman*
Mr.Wrong/Mr.Right-
Ogili-*A local spice*
Yesmah/Nosemah-*Yes Mam/No sir*
Ube-*Pear*

Ogwogwo mmili takumei ayolo-*A kind of African children's rain song or rhyme.*
Mother Idoto-*Mother figure in some African myths.*

Chapter 8

This chapter is narrated through the myth of Idemili. This Igbo goddess is sent by the Almighty, to *"bear witness to the moral nature of authority by wrapping around power's rude waist a loincloth of peace and modesty"*. This goddess is personified as water. The importance of Idemili is underscored by the rites anybody who wants the Ozo chieftaincy title must follow. Such a person must be accompanied by a female in getting this title. This myth is used to illustrate how raw, absolute power must be mellowed by feminine attributes enshrined in Idemili.

Beatrice begins to ruminate on her personality. She sees herself as possessing dual personality of a human being and a priestess. Achebe captures a typical priestess as portrayed in Beatrice. *"... the village priestess who will prophesy when her divinity rides her abandoning if need be her soup-pot on the fire, but returning again when the god departs to the domesticity of kitchen..."*. As a priestess, she is expected to possess some prophetic powers and this is not lacking in Beatrice. At the height of the cold-war between Chris and Ikem, she prophetically utters, *"And I see trouble building up for us. It will get to Ikem first. No joking, Chris. He will be the precursor to make straight the way. But after him it will be you...You and Ikem must quickly patch up this ridiculous thing between you that nobody has ever been able to explain to me."*

Beatrice reminisces on her experience during her invitation to the President's dinner. Chris later visits and Beatrice confronts him with the accusation of indifference by allowing her to attend the Presidential dinner. *"I am the girl you say you want to marry...O.K. am taken away in strange circumstances...You come here and all you say to me is: don't worry, it's all right"*. Chris could not defend himself against this accusation, but he is able to lovingly cuddle her and their relationship is further strengthened. However, the fear of the onslaught of the government on its perceived enemies becomes stronger

Commentary

This chapter introduces the use of myth in the storytelling style of Achebe. Though Idemili is a local Igbo heroine, the author is able to weave universal contents round her. The symbolic nomenclature of water to depict Idemili creates a picture of restraint on the unbridled strength of power, especially in the mould of a tyrant like the President. This re-echoes the popular words of President Jefferson, *"Power corrupts, absolute power corrupts absolutely"*. The issue also stresses the imperativeness of women participation in governance.

The opinion of Beatrice as a dual figure is strengthened. Though late to be introduced in the story, she is systematically being made to evolve from the shadows of the men into a dominant figure. While the male characters possess a mono-personality, she is imbued with prophetic strength. By the end of the chapter, the force of opposition as composed in Chris and Beatrice is waiting in anticipation of the onslaught of the government.

GLOSSARY
Ozo-*A chieftaincy title in Igboland.*
Nwakibie-*A powerful son*
Adire- *A tie and die textile design.*
Onyeka Onwenu's One Love-*A musical album by a Nigerian female artist.*

Chapter 9
Ikem decides to visit the elders of Abazon who are in Harmony Hotel. He discovers on his arrival that the elders are just six, but are now joined by some indigenes of Abazon resident in Bassa. He is warmly welcomed by the elders who shower praises on him for his gallant defence of the rights of the common men in his writings. The spokesman for the elders speaks extensively on various issues especially on how to go about the struggle against dictatorship. According to him and speaking from experience, *story* would win the fight against oppression better than battle. He speaks extensively on the enduring power of *words*:

> *Recalling –is-Greatest. Why? Because it is only the story that can continue beyond the war and warrior. It is the story that outlives the sound of war-drums and the exploits of brave fighters. It is the story, not the others ,that saves our progeny from blundering like blind beggars into the spikes of the cactus fence…It is the thing that makes us different from cattle; it is the mark on the face that sets one people apart from their neighbours.*

The elder thereafter reveals how Ikem has been instrumental to the people of Abazon not voting in support of the life presidency ambition of the President. He tacitly refers to the new approach of the people of Abazon. *"So we came to Bassa to say our own yes and perhaps the work on our boreholes will start again and we will not all perish from the anger of the sun. So we are ready to learn new things and mend our old useless ways."* With his speech laced with many anecdotes, myths and proverbs, the elderly speaker ends his talk on a conciliatory note *'My people, that is all we are doing now. Struggling. Perhaps to no purpose except that those who come after us will be able to say: True, our fathers were defeated but they tried"*.

On leaving, it is obvious that Ikem has been trailed by the agents of the President to the venue. When he is about to drive off, he suffers the first intimidation from a police officer who charges him for a traffic offence for not putting on his *"parking light"*. He is later cleared and apologized to at the police station by a Superintendent, but one thing is clear, the phantom indictment of Ikem for a traffic offence would later be used as an excuse against him for having attended the meeting with the elders of Abazon.

Commentary

The author presents Ikem in his first activist manner. The fact that this chapter comes after Chris and Beatrice have exercised some concern on the impending onslaught of the President against the opposition, makes this scene quite significant. There is a symbolic meeting of minds between a modern ilk in the person of Ikem and the traditional elements represented by the Abazon elders. This unity shows the concerted effort that is always needed to fight dictatorship. The elder's ode on the power of words echoes the power of the press to be a responsive one to the aspirations of the people, rather than being used as a tool in the hands of oppressors. The elder's words also echo one of the ideals of Achebe as a writer in his belief in reform and subtle agitation rather than violent revolution in fighting dictatorship. The diplomacy and tact of the elders of Abazon is instructive. They would, *"learn the new ways"*, rather than all die from starvation from the vindictiveness of the President. The *"anger of the sun"* which the elder mentions unravels the mystery of Ikem's *"Hymn to the Sun"* in chapter three. The identity of the sun is clearly aligned with all its omnipotence to the President.

GLOSSARY
Chi-*God*
Iroko-*A hard brown African wood often used instead of teak.*
Ukwa-*Breadfruit*
Na me-*It is me*
Gbali-gbali-*A query*

Chapter 10
With the humiliation suffered by Ikem in the hands of police officers in the previous chapter, appreciation for his role in nation building comes early enough when two taxi drivers come to visit him. One of them is the driver who drives Elewa home in chapter four. They are visiting to apologize for the way one of them has treated Ikem during a traffic congestion incident and also to appreciate him for his fight for the masses in his writings. Ikem, in return, apologizes and they shake hands as a sign of friendship.

After the visit, Ikem drives to Mad Medico's house but on the way he begins to ruminate on the visit of the drivers. He feels appreciated for what he has been doing and for the uneducated drivers to particularly mention an incident when his editorial has influenced a government policy, is quite humbling for Ikem. He is however puzzled by the expectations of the taxi drivers concerning his standard of living:
...how does one begin to explain the downtrodden drivers' wistful preference for a leader driving not like themselves in a battered and spluttering vehicle but differently, stylishly in a Mercedes and better still with another downtrodden person like themselves for a chauffeur?

The same theme is captured by the poem of David Diop in the opening poem of the chapter:

Africa tell me Africa
Is this you this back this is bent
This back that breaks under the weight of humiliation

Ikem then tries to proffer a solution to an African mind that is slavishly submissive and filled with hero-worship tendencies: *"Therefore what is at issue in all this may only be alleviated by a good spread of general political experience, slow of growth and obstinately patient like the young..."*

When Ikem seeks Elewa's perception on the issue, she seems to share the opinion of the drivers that a leader should be celebrated and elevated above his followers. In her words, *"I no tell you that before say this kind car wey you get de make person shame"*

Commentary
In the chapter before this, Ikem is vilified and harassed under a flimsy excuse of traffic offence from a government that is supposed to appreciate and possibly reward him, but in this chapter, he gets the accolade he deserves from the members of the lower class. This brings into perspective the class war between the bourgeoisie and the proletariat. Ikem ruminates on the contradiction of why the oppressed may not be able to fight their oppressors. There is an expectation of opulence and status which an oppressed person wants to see in his oppressor even if done at his own expense. In offering a solution to this malady, Ikem seems to speak the mind of Achebe on the need for a systematic orientation and reform of the people's psyche.

GLOSSARY
Jagajaga-*Rubbish*
Datsun-*A brand of car*
Dachas-*A Russian cottage or house in the suburbs or countryside.*

Chapter 11
Ikem once again savours the exhilaration of the appreciation shown by the taxi drivers. He longs for camaraderie with this class of people, but he realizes that while someone like Elewa could have such experience, he is somehow ostracized. He contemplates the decadence in the Kangan government.

In another scene, the President calls Sam into his office and orders him to suspend Ikem from his position as the Editor of the *National Gazette* for having met with the elders of Abazon. Chris who could not see the correlation between Ikem's meeting with the Abazon elders and the suspension he is being expected to issue him, rejects the President's order .The President is thereafter forced to reveal his grievance against Ikem and even Chris for being disloyal and influencing the people of Abazon to vote against his Life Presidency ambition in a past referendum. Exasperated, Chris decides to resign his own appointment as the

Commissioner for Information. The President rejects this and he subtly threatens Chris, *"We will take it from here. Meanwhile, the SRC Director will be chatting with you on a number of leads he has developed on the bungling of the referendum and other matters..."* Subsequently, Ikem is suspended by a phantom Chairman, Board of Directors of Kangan Newspapers Corporation. In a meeting with Chris, Ikem and Beatrice in attendance, they begin to discuss the latest development and how they prepare themselves for the impending assault of the dictatorial President. They all later heard that the six elders of Abazon have been arrested and this really sets Ikem on edge.

Commentary
This chapter presents a systematic build up to the climax of the novel as the President and his agents begin to bare their fangs. From the excitement of Ikem on his appreciation by the masses represented by the taxi drivers, he is subsequently faced with the persecution of the ruling class. Beatrice with her prophetic insight is able to have the last laugh, *"Well, I still think that if you and Chris had listened to me and stopped your running battles as you call them early enough, he would not now trying to disgrace you"*. However for the first time in the novel, a unifying force is being created by Ikem, Chris, Beatrice, and even Elewa to confront the impending offensive of the government. The chapter ends on a speedy and expectant note of the confrontation ahead.

Chapter 12
Now that Ikem has been relieved of his position as the Editor of the government-owned *National Gazette,* he now seems to have all the freedom. The opportunity presents itself when he is invited to give a talk in the University of Bassa. Ikem's lecture is entitled, *"The Tortoise and the Leopard"*. It is during the Question Time that Ikem is able to express his philosophies on various controversial issues. For example, he condemns the desirability of democratic dictatorship which most people would easily embrace. In his argument, there is no particular class of people that can be referred to as peasants per se. He equally condemns the decadence that has pervaded all classes of people, no matter their social class. The speaker advocates instead what he calls *'new radicalism'* He expatiates:

> *This radicalism must be clear-eyed enough to see beyond the present claptrap that will heap all our problems on the doorstep of capitalism and imperialism...But you cannot do that unless you first set about to purge yourselves, to clean up your act. You must learn for a start to hold your own student leaders to responsible performance*

The questions begin as Ikem excitedly answers them.

Commentary

This chapter marks the first opportunity for Ikem to openly share his beliefs and philosophies on pressing national issues with the people in the street. Though under a military regime, he is able to give full vent to the real meaning of freedom of expression.

Just as the government is planning its own attack, the opposition too is not folding its arms. Ikem's call for a sense of responsibility instead of buck-passing is very significant. As if speaking the mind of Achebe, he refuses to blame neo-colonialism or even any political system as the bane of underdevelopment in Africa. Rather, Ikem seems to place the ingredients of change in the hands of the youths represented as students here.

Chapter 13

One of the questions asked Ikem at the University of Bassa Talk is his response to the rumour going the round that the President's image is about to be put on the national currency. He innocently answers, "...*any serving President foolish enough to lay his head on a coin should know he is inciting people to take it off; the head I mean*". The following day the *National Gazettte* entitles this: EX-EDITOR ADVOCATES REGICIDE.

In the aftermath of Ikem's lecture which has been termed an open challenge to the government, Mad Medico is summarily deported to his home country under a flimsy reason. The President's hatchet man, Major Ossai is promoted to the rank of a full colonel.

All this development gets Chris and Beatrice worried about the safety of Ikem and they begin to look for him. On the visit to Ikem's house, the neighbours reveal that some men in uniform had come and had forcefully abducted Ikem putting him in hand-cuffs. The search continues until the government makes an announcement, that an investigation has linked Ikem with the *"kangan Plotters"* and that he has incited the people against the government. The release further claims that in an attempt to arrest Ikem a scuffle results and is *"fatally wounded by gunshot"*. For Chris he knows that the government has murdered Ikem and if he does not escape, he may be the next target. The government begins the search for Chris as he moves from one hide-out to another.

Commentary

The first major build up to the climax of the story begins. The President that had earlier displayed some amount of restraint appears to have been suddenly woken from its slumber by the open challenge of Ikem. The intolerance and the sense of insecurity of the government are openly displayed here. It takes mere words to shake the credibility of the government. This echoes the words of the chief spokesman of the elders of Abazon in chapter 9 *"Because it is only the story that outlives the sound of war drums"*. The same view has been expressed by Ikem in chapter 4, *"Our best weapon against them is not to marshal facts, of which they are truly managers, but passion"*

The murder of Ikem under gruesome circumstances shows the brutality of a military dictatorship and the manipulation of government agencies (the Press) to perpetrate its totalitarian grip on the state.

The high point of the chapter is the coming together of all the people regarded as the *"dregs of the society"* such as the taxi drivers and even the students, who resist the attempt by the mobile policeman to arrest the President and the Secretary of the Student Union. This incident fulfils the call of Ikem in the University of Bassa, that the ingredients for change in the society are inherent in the masses.

GLOSSARY
Koboko-*Horse whip*
Valium-*A kind of sedative*
Pickin-*Child*

Chapter 14

Beatrice receives an anonymous phone call asking her to move Chris to another location for safety purpose, *"Get him moved Before tonight"*. She becomes confused as she could not ascertain the authenticity of the caller. In the turmoil around her, she loses her bunch of keys, but finds it later. In the taxi she enters, she discovers that all taxi drivers are about to go on strike to protest the murder of Ikem. On returning home, Beatrice had a quarrel with Agatha, her home help over her treatment of Elewa, who she feels does not deserve her respect because of her social class and the kind of respect and attention she gets from the like of Beatrice. Beatrice could not fathom the rationale behind Agatha's religious piety. *"Yes, this Agatha who was so free with leaflets dripping with the saving blood of Jesus and yet had no single drop of charity in her own anaemic blood".* In Beatrice's reflection, she begins to appreciate the inner beauty of Elewa which radiates above her social class. This beauty must have attracted Ikem to her. Beatrice however decides to reconcile with Agatha by apologizing to her for the manner she has treated her and *"the unbelief turned first to shock and then, through the mist of tears, a sunrise of smiles."* By the end of the chapter, Agatha has joined the *"struggle"* as she too prays for the safety of Chris.

The government's search for Chris continues and the government resorts to different propaganda, of Chris' flight in disguise to London, having been involved in a coup plot. The government declares him wanted.

Commentary

The consolidation of the masses to fight the hegemony and oppression of the military dictatorship in the land is implied here. The news of the taxi drivers who want *"to put their mouth into this nonsense story of Ikem's death"* is revolutionary.

Shortly after, Beatrice is able to take a critical look at the self-imposed bondage Agatha has put herself into in the name of religion. Beatrice feels she deserves compassion, understanding and love instead of criticism, and condemnation. When Beatrice does this, she could see a transformation in Agatha as *"through tears, a sunrise of smiles rises".* The accommodation of Agatha into the struggle fold is evident in her prayer for Chris' protection by the end of the chapter.

The desperate and dirty tactics of Sam in weaving lies round Chris and finally declaring him wanted is akin to the machinations that surround the disappearance of Ikem.

GLOSSARY

Boys Quarter-*The back of a flat meant for maids/homehelps*
Amin-Na so we talk-*Amen...that is our wish.*

Chapter 15

Chris continues in moving from one hide-out to another and his last place is a Boy's Quarter, but his host feels that he may no longer be safe with them, so it is decided that Chris move out of the GRA, where he is currently quartered for *"the northern slum"* in the house of Braimoh, the taxi driver.

Emmanuel, the President of the Student Union, who is also on the wanted list of the government joins Chris in hiding. As a decoy, Emmanuel places a news article in the *National Gazette* about Chris escaping to London. In his eyes, the ease with which he places the news casts aspersion on the Press in Kangan. Later, Chris begins his journey to the Far North, having escaped some police check-points.

Commentary

It is significant to note that Chris gets help from the so-called commoners in the society such as the taxi drivers and even the student leader. It is ironic that the ruling class that Chris has served is the one hunting him. He must have realized that he is finally in the company of people that he really belongs: the masses. Does this situate the hope of redemption in the proletariat? This chapter also casts more reservation on the effectiveness of government agencies such as the Police and even the press under a dictatorial military regime. An ordinary citizen like Emmanuel easily place a fictitious story, which the paper did not attempt to verify. The police are not better off.

GLOSSARY

Make you dey chew am for road...*Continue to chew it as you journey on.*
Dem two na my people...-*The two people are well known to me.*
Original and Taiwan-*Original and fake.*

Chapter 16

Chris begins the journey to the North. The choice of Abazon as a sanctuary is significant for many reasons. It is Ikem's, *"native province"...It is also the distant sustainer of all his best inspirations"*. Abazon is equally regarded as the bastion of opposition to the military regime. Braimoh's wife Aina is also from this part of the country.

On the night of Chris' departure, Beatrice decides to spend what she considers the last night with her fiancé. Chris shows his altruistic self when he forbids the children being *"ejected from their floor because of Beatrice"*. He would also not abuse the sensibilities of his host by spraying aerosol into their mosquito-infested room. The following day, Chris, Emmanuel and Buraimoh proceed on their journey to Abazon.

Commentary

The tone of Chris is already tainted with premonition of an impending tragedy for him. Beatrice has symbolically come and spent what may be their last night together. Even in the midst of this obvious tension, Chris is able to exhibit his altruistic nature. He detests a situation where they would send the children of Buraimoh away from the room, where he and Beatrice would sleep just because of privacy. He is even more sensitive to the sensibilities of a person of Buraimoh's social status. He would rather endure mosquito bite than buy aerosol to disinfect the room where they would sleep. *"...aerosol was a remedy our host could not himself afford it was perhaps better not to insult him by introducing it into his household"*. Could one claim that these altruistic actions from Chris are borne out of a sense of guilt of having fought against the interest of the masses as Commissioner for Information? Or is it that the influence of Sam's shadow has robbed Chris of any sense of responsibility to the masses?

GLOSSARY
GRA-*Government Residential Area*
Lappa-*Clothing wrapper*
Luxurious-*Luxury bus.*
Ife onye metalu-*Nemesis*

Chapter 17

As Chris begins his journey, he observes the obvious neglect of this part of the country by the government as a form of punishment for Abazon's rebellion and opposition .On the condition of the road, the author writes, *"Even the asphalt on which **Luxurious** sped towards the North told its own story of two countries. Thickly-laid and cushiony at first it steadily deteriorated into thin black paint applied with niggardly strokes..."*.Even the buildings are not as imposing as those found in the Southern part of the country.

As they progress in their journey, it is Braimoh who observes a large crowd, and on getting closer, they find more and more people in an exhilarating mood, celebrating with bottles of beer. In their investigation, they discover that there has been a coup d'etat and *"the President don disappear"*. With this news, Chris and the others decide to return to Bassa, but Chris had to intervene in a scuffle where a police sergeant attempts to rape a girl. In the fray, Chris is shot point blank by the policeman.

Commentary
The title of this chapter appropriately tagged, "Great" spells the climax of the entire novel. The celebration that greets the overthrow of the President demonstrates the common people's disaffection with the autocratic regime of Sam. Poetic justice seems to play itself out here. The way he is abducted is the same manner the President disappears. In the midst of this euphoria, which would have marked a triumphant victory for Chris as he prepares to return to liberty, something tragic happens. Chris is unceremoniously shot dead. This marks the climax of the entire story. This incident is riddled with many ironies. In running from Bassa, which he considers to be an unsafe place, he walks into his death in a place which the author has described as where *"you could count on having your secrets kept secret"*. However, in running from one soldier, he ends up in the hand of another unscrupulous policeman. Chris' death is probably avoidable, but he only continues on his altruistic path of defending the helpless, especially the womenfolk. He surrenders himself sacrificially and tragically, not to the sword of the government, but that of a social system whose dynamics is warped. A police officer that is supposed to protect, ends being the predator.

GLOSSARY
How the go de go?-*How is everything?*
Egusi soup-*A kind of local soup made from melon.*
Bush meat-*Game*
Very Desent Restorant-*A Very Decent Restaurant.*
Na proper tug -of –war-*It is a real tug of war.*
Harmattan-*An extremely dry dusty wind that blows from the Sahara toward the western coast of Africa, between November and March every year.*
So at the same time we hear…to make our own cocktail party-*As the news of the coup d'etat was filtering in, that was when this lorry filled with beer was passing and we learnt that it belonged to the government, but now that the government has been overthrown, we saw it as our own windfall to have our cocktail party.*
IMF-*International Monetary Fund*

Chapter 18

Beatrice decides to call all her friends together and name the newly born child of late Ikem and Elewa, since the elders from Elewa's family have decided to boycott the Naming Ceremony. The stoic manner Beatrice bears the loss of Chris is also shown. She gets inspired from Elewa's threatened abortion. For her, it is worth all the efforts to keep the living alive than selfishly mourn the dead. She reminisces on the state of the country, where with the ascendancy of the new military ruler, nothing has really changed. Rather, she derives succour from her new set of friends- Emmanuel, Adamma (the lady Chris saved from being raped), Agatha, Captain Abdul Bedani, Braimoh and his wife, Aina, all from different backgrounds, yet joined in love and the struggle to see a better society. The child is finally given the name *Amaechina* (may the path never close) a propitious reference to the continuation of Ikem's progeny and ideals. However, later and surprisingly, Elewa's uncle and mother appear. While the uncle decides to take a different course of cooperation with Beatrice and the rest, the mother remains adamant. The uncle refuses to condemn the so-called desecration of custom, which gives a woman the right to name a child. In his words *"...in you young people our world has met its match. Yes! You have put the world where it should sit".* After the ceremony, Emmanuel let slip the last words of Chris, "the last Grin" which Beatrice corrects to be "The Last Green (Bottle). This statement brings a new found consolation into the mind of Beatrice that Chris dies a happy, contented man, even shaming death as against her own father who died cowardly.

Commentary

While the opening chapter of the novel begins in a male dominated world of Sam' Cabinet, the closing chapter ends in a female –dominated world. Elewa's family decides to boycott the Naming Ceremony on many grounds, ranging from the absence of the new baby's father to the child itself being born out of a properly conducted wedding.

The radical posture of Beatrice taking the initiative to commence the ceremony without the presence of the elders shows the new role the women have come to play in the novel especially the roles that Achebe feels they should play. In the absence of the male heroes i.e. Chris and Ikem, it behoves Beatrice with the mental strength to continue with the struggle. This continuity also extends to the name given to the new baby,

Ameachina-*May -the- path -never- close*. It speaks of the continuity of Ikem's legacy.

The spirit of feminism is also celebrated here as attested to by Braimoh, *'I think our tradition is faulty there. It is really safest to ask the mother what her child is or means or should be called"*. This view vindicates the initiative of Beatrice in continuing with the naming ceremony even without the presence of elders. While this may appear as an aberration culture-wise, its pragmatism tallies with the progressiveness of this new modern age, devoid of religious bigotry, ethnic chauvinism and class jingoism or consciousness. While Elewa's mother is *"left high and dry carrying the anger of outraged custom..."* Beatrice leads the vanguard of progressiveness not totally doing away with African culture but finding a meeting point of virtues for both cultures. In the end, Elewa's mother *"...opened her bag and handed a kolanut to him",* an attestation of her acceptance of the synergy of the two cultures.

At the end of the ceremony, the novel is brought to a befitting end with the revelation of Emmanuel of the last words of Chris at the point of death, *"the Last Green"*, which Beatrice later fully spells out as the *"The Last Green Bottle"*. For Beatrice, the consolation is that Chris has shamed death by laughing it to scorn, unlike her own father who fears death with all morbidity.

Though the future may appear bleak, there is the hope in the seed of Ikem, Amechina, and even in the new group headed by Beatrice, where the common goal is to see to the uplift of the human race without any room for racial discrimination, political leaning, religious loyalty and cultural bondage.

GLOSSARY
Coup d'etat-*the sudden violent overthrow of a government and seizure of political power, especially by the military*
Soja come, soja gwo-*Soldiers come and they also go*
Na true my brother-*You are right my brother.*
Inyanga-*Show off.*
Na yeye father we be-*We are irresponsible fathers indeed.*
I no shy but I no sabi book-*I am not shy, but I am not literate.*
Dis no be book matter-*It is not a question of being literate.*
...to show your sufferhead-*A reward for all your pains.*
Ise-*Amen*

CHINUA ACHEBE'S STYLE AND LANGUAGE

Achebe's *Anthills of the Savannah* could be considered experimental in the annals of his literary history. The language compared to others is elevated and almost poetic. The characters are well-developed, sophisticated intellectuals who are acquainted with all the dynamics of the 21st century world. Though one could locate the setting as being that of Nigeria, yet the issues explored transcend the Nigerian border, highlighting issues generic to the African continent as a whole and even, at times, with universal consequence.

It would therefore be right to assert that, the work is a culmination of all the ideals of Achebe's as a writer. The book still explores some of the narrative styles and language that have often given Achebe his identity as a writer.

One outstanding style in *Anthills of the Savannah* is the modernist writing of Stream of Consciousness. Narration does not follow a logical path, but rather non-liner. Great demands are placed on the reader or the audience who have to contend with abundance of detailed descriptions and the onus often rests on the reader to decide the importance of each. Achebe continuously shifts narrators ranging from Ikem, Chris and Beatrice whose views are presented, allowing the reader to choose the most truthful perspective. This modernist style often ignores strict chronology. Ideas are expressed as they flow into the mind. The thought-interlude is used on page 27 where a paragraph on the *Sun* is presented. The full version is later shown on page 30 under the title, *Hymn to the Sun*, a write-up by Ikem, which he writes on reaching home after a hard day under the scorching April sun.

This literary style is linked to the copious use of flashback in the novel. Achebe uses the intellectuals in the novel as the fulcrum of this technique. Thoughts explored by Ikem, Chris and Beatrice are very enriching and intellectually stimulating. These characters are the leaders of thoughts in the novel. A character like Elewa did not use flashback for once in the novel. Though the story line may at times appear convoluted, the use of flashback has many benefits. It gives more insight into the personality of the characters involved. Flashbacks also shed more light on the experience of a character at a particular time. Reasons are given for some knotty issues. After Ikem has sent Elewa away, he ruminates on the reason he behaves as he does, not allowing his girlfriend to spend the night with him. Ikem's attitude towards womanhood generally is explored.

Story telling is also an integral part of the styles in the novel. Though set in an urban area, some elders such as those of Abazon and even the uncle of Elewa are often presented as repository of African wisdom. Though issues narrated by these elders are African in context, yet they have contemporary relevance. Folktale is used by the Chief spokesman for the Abazons who narrates the *Leopard and Tortoise* story. Storytelling must have been something admirable to an intellectual like Ikem who borrows the *Leopard and the Tortoise* story as the fulcrum of his lecture at the University of Bassa. The Idemili story in chapter 8 borrows a myth to find a basis for a universal concept. The water-personality of the goddess Idemili is portrayed as a feminine calming effect in a fiery masculine world.

The stories are not isolated but imbued with didactic proverbs and other traditional maxims, which are copiously used by elders in the novel. The economy and humour elicited by these proverbs add richness to the narrative. *"…a man who answers every summons by the town-crier will not plant corn on his fields"* is a proverb in defence of Ikem not being available to interact with his kinsmen due to his more demanding vocation as a journalist. A humorous one is, *"when a rich man is sick a beggar goes to visit him and say sorry. When the beggar is sick, he waits to recover and then goes to tell the rich man that he has been sick"*, which stresses the gap between two social classes, the ruler and the ruled.

Language is used as a social distinction tool in the novel. A character with low education such as Elewa uses Pidgin English, and with all its brashness, she is able to express herself without the inhibition of the Upper Class. Sam and the members of his cabinet and even Ikem speak Queen's English in view of their British educational background. Med Medico, though a Briton, seems to derive much power of expression in even Pidgin English. It becomes a veritable tool to express his sarcasm. He is so enamored of his Houseboy's inspirational statement that he has the inscription on top of his bar:

ALL THE BEER
DEM DRINK FOR HERE
DE MAKE ME FEAR

The ambiguity Achebe appears to create is to make the African elders speak English language. Being the language of expression in the novel, this is imperative. However, one could decipher that the elders such as the chief spokesman for the Abazon people and even the uncle of Elewa speak in their native tongues considering the richness of their language in terms of proverbs, anecdotes, maxims and incisive use of African native wisdom which English language would have been inadequate to capture or express.

In addition, Achebe explores the use of symbolic association and imagery to profess some concepts in the novel. The visit of the Abazon people is appropriately described as a *storm* and placed against the background of a stormy weather. *"Over and beyond the roof the tops of palm-trees at the waterfront swayed with the same lazy ease they display to gentle ocean winds. It was no ordinary storm".* This insidious incident, slowly gathers momentum to be the storm that eventually sweeps all the three gladiators-Ikem, Chris and Sam away by the end of the novel.

The image of the *Sun* is well utilized in the *Hymn to the Sun* written by Ikem. Though written in form of appeasing the ferociousness of the April heat, yet it captures the essence of Sam's personality who with his dictatorial power has become as omnipotent as the *Sun* itself, which could scorch any opposition to submission.

Achebe's elevated language drawing largely from poetic vigour is worthy of note. The imagery is vivid enough to appeal to all senses. This is the sort of language that runs through the entire novel. *"Hymn to the Sun"* exemplifies this:

> *Household animals were all dead. First pigs fried in their own fat; and when the sheep and goats and cattle choked by their swollen tongues.*
> *Stray dogs in the market-place in a running battle with vultures devoured the corpse of the madman they found at last coiled up one morning in the stall over which he had assumed unbroken tenancy and from where he had sallied forth every morning...*

The beauty of Achebe's style and language is the ability to use the vehicle of African tongue and norms to express contemporary issues of universal significance. This shows his belief in the merger of the virtues in African culture with that of the Western world.

THE CHARACTERS

Sam
Your Excellency is always right

He is the military ruler of an African state, Kangan and as it is expected of his mode of ascension, he rules by military fiat and dictatorship becomes the rule. Sam is a model of a typical African military Head of State.

He is the first speaker in the novel with his autocratic tone *"...Finish Kabisa! Any other business",* showing clearly who is in charge. He definitely does not allow any dissenting voice and this intolerance would set him on a collision with his friends especially Chris who is a member of his cabinet. In the typical mould of an African monarch, Sam remains the object of veneration and adulation to his commissioners who have to feel his mood before making any statement. Sycophancy becomes the order of the day among the commissioners, that have to jostle for attention by backbiting and maligning each other.

Sam comes to power through a coup and as such does not derive his authority and legitimacy from the people. This probably explains his isolationist tendencies throughout the story. A mere solidarity visit by the people of Abazon is enough to create some panic for him. Because he is not people-oriented, he lacks the empathy of a true leader. He would rather be caught speaking to the President of the United States of America than go to meet the Abazon people. In maintaining this isolation, he further indulges in lies and duplicity to cover his tracks. His instruction to Professor Okong on how to manage the media coverage is interesting, *'But for God's sake, Professor, I want you to look at the man you are shaking hands with instead of the camera'* Interestingly, the same level of duplicity seems to have been imbibed by his subordinates. The decadence and rot at the top hierarchy have a way of percolating to the lowest rung of the ladder.

Though he may not be trained for rulership, Sam is not as dull as anybody may think. He has a way of getting the right information from his subordinates with his boosted ego intact. His character reading ability is shown in his ability see through the sycophancy of Professor Okong who thinks he has made an impression on his boss when he has ironically made a fool of himself. Chris confirms this talent of Sam '...*he has a knack for reading faces*'.

In the manner of a typical dictator, Sam's disdain for intellectual power is obvious in the novel. He shows this trait when he describes Professor Okong, '*And he calls himself a university professor. No wonder they say he now heads a handclapping spiritualist congregation on campus. Disgraceful. Soft to the core, that's what they all are. Professor!*' The paradox for Sam is that the friends he surrounds himself with such as Ikem, Mad Medico and even Chris are all intellectual libertines. Sam must have cultivated the friendship of these people to learn the ropes from them on coming to power, and having mastered the acts of statesmanship, he finds it difficult to tolerate their cerebral bluntness.

Despite his façade of infallibility, Sam could be naïve at times. He worships anything Anglicism up to the point of foolishness. He relishes the aristocratic life style of the English Upper with its pleasure, yet could not embrace the democratic standard of the Europeans. He has to remind Chris when he threatens to resign his appointment that he is not in Westminster or Washington DC. In his visit to the OAU meeting, he is reduced to a baby awed by the antics of the elderly. The only word he seems to have gained is *Kabisa* and his admiration of a taciturn sit-tight, notorious Head of State.

Sam grows from a gentleman to a monster when he actually bares his full fangs. The visit of the Abazon elders at the opening paragraph becomes his albatross by the end of the story. He plots the murder of Ikem, hunts Chris to his demise and repatriates Mad Medico all in the bid to have a total hold on the state of Kangan. By the end of the novel when he is assassinated, he becomes more inconsequential especially when one considers the fact that another soldier takes over the government with obviously no immediate hope for democratic emergence.

Chris
I don't think Chris is one hundred percent behind you

He is first introduced through his position as the Commissioner for Information in Sam's Cabinet. He, however, stands out from the rest. He is ever ready to tell the President the truth without any guise of sycophancy. Sam must have appreciated this candour at the inception of their friendship, but by the time Sam has consolidated his reign, Chris becomes his number one threat.

Chris' dilemma is often shown in his view of the role of the press in Kangan. Should the press be on the side of the people or on the side of the ruling government? For Chris, he has to contend with protecting the interest of his boss cum friend as against his personal philosophy of democratic principles. This puts him on collusion course with Ikem on a number of times.

Chris' sensitivity must have been aroused by Ikem who tries to make him understand that the press should be on the side of the people .It takes the President's order for Chris to issue a sack letter to Ikem to make him make up his mind which side he would stand. This decisive moment and realization makes Chris to confront Sam and he refuses to sack Ikem. He even decides to drop his own letter. This courage marks Chris out as a conscientious fighter.

It is as if Chris feels some remorse about betraying the people's trust and he strives to gain time to atone for this, unlike Ikem who has always made the people's cause his vocation.

Chris begins by showing his altruistic spirit by being reluctant and disallowing Braimoh's children from vacating the room for himself and Beatrice, so that they can have their privacy. He goes further to show his sensitive side by now allowing a disinfectant to be used in the same house as this may embarrass the sensitivity of his host.

The irony of Chris' demise is that running to safety, he eventually runs into his unfortunate death in the hands of a trigger-happy policeman. Here again, he makes the final atonement for the defence of the defenceless Adamma, who is about to be raped and everybody looks on with insouciance. This is one of the banes of Kangan, when nobody sees it as his responsibility to confront oppression under any guise. Chris does it sacrificially for Adamma and he dies contented. This gives Beatrice a satisfying memory which she would live with the rest of her life. Her memory of Chris is not that of a wasted life, but somebody who is courageous enough to laugh death itself to scorn. *'But look at Chris, a young man with all his life in front of him and yet he was able to look death in the eyes and smile and make joke .It was too wonderful...'*

Ikem
But Ikem is a literary artist...

He is the pure intellectual libertine in the novel. Incidentally, he is a friend of the President and this puts him in an uncomfortable position of balancing loyalty between conscience and friendship. Unlike Chris, he is able to realize on time where he really stands and it is on the side of the people. His position as the Editor of the *National Gazette* makes him the quintessential symbol of expression and press freedom in the novel.

His personal lifestyle may, however, be at variance with what he preaches. He loves humanity, yet lacks the capability of appreciating womanhood. This is shown in his reaction to Elewa. Ikem would find it convenient to savour the sexual pleasure that Elewa offers, but would hesitate to take the responsibility that goes with it. Beatrice attests to Ikem's attitude towards women, *"Ikem doesn't say much to any girl. He doesn't think they have enough brains".*

What marks Ikem out among other characters is his intellectual energy, which he disposes for the benefit of his fellow humans especially the downtrodden. He is the symbol of the struggle of the people of Abazon. Though he might not have physically incited the people of the area to vote NO in the referendum that would have made Sam Life President, the people recognize him as an opinion leader whose views should be followed and that is exactly what they do at critical moments. Ikem's editorial on capital punishment is somehow instrumental to the abrogation of the practice. Even the taxi drivers are grateful for his writings, which influence the government, of the hygienic state of their bus station.

The radical bend of Ikem could sometimes make him unrealistic. He could not see why Chris could not oppose Sam despite serving under him. This leads to their conflicts on a number of times.

The end of Ikem is characteristic of his personality. He abhors dictatorship, inequality and oppression under any guise. Having been relieved of his position as the Editor, he feels he has got the leeway to give full vent to his ideals and philosophy. At the University of Bassa, he is able to chart the course for Kangan's future. He would not lay the blame for the decadence in Kangan at the footstep of neo-colonialism or even a particular social class, rather, he calls for individual responsibility to make a change in the society. This consciousness must have changed the life of Emmanuel, making him more responsible and in the course of the novel becoming more involved in the struggle against dictatorship.

As a martyr of the struggle, Ikem leaves many legacies behind. His murder under questionable circumstances somehow sparks off the storm that eventually sweeps Sam away. With his death, the taxi drivers embark on strike. Chris is able to regain his consciousness on the need to make a stand. At his death, Ikem has given birth to two children, namely Emmanuel and Amaechina and in death, Beatrice is able to come to the realization that all of them, with the same mind and aspirations should come together, no matter their backgrounds to forge a common front to liberate their society.

Beatrice
Nwanyibuife-A female is also something

Beatrice –BB is a major character whose strength is anchored on her intellectual vigour, understanding of feminine power, self-awareness and strong leadership qualities.

She is the calming influence in the novel. She tries many times to reconcile the two friends, Ikem and Chris on the need for them to forge a formidable front to fight the opposition instead of dissipating their energy in fighting each other. Beatrice is even more convincing and interesting because of her prophetic vigour. She sees the onslaught of Sam before it happens.

Beatrice's pride in her femininity is shown during her invitation to the Presidential Retreat, which she views as an aspersion on her person. She could not fathom why the President would use her as a mere window dressing tool to impress the foreign visitors. This incident for her, underscores the way women are used as a mere decoration in an African society.

She is a typical self-made person who has explored the opportunities that are available to lift herself to the pedestal of professional excellence where she finds herself. Here is a person that would have been stifled by her parental discrimination, being an unwanted female child and even the chauvinistic attitude of her male-dominated society. She surmounts all these with her unequalled courage to be a woman of substance. All these experiences must have armed her as the bastion of women empowerment and emancipation.

Beatrice is often described as a priestess. Apart from the prophetic power implied her, she is also imbued with healing virtues. She is able to understand the loneliness of Agatha who is equally bound in religious fanaticism and instead of unleashing vengeance on her, Beatrice discovers that all she needs is compassion and once she could do this, Agatha is brought into the fold. It takes the compassion of Beatrice to heal Elewa of her bereavement. She nurtures her and her baby and literally adopts them as her own. This humanist posture is commendable as a true leader. This attribute is also explored by the end of the story when Beatrice becomes the rallying point for Emmanuel, Adamma and the rest in charting a new course for the future.

In her role as the rallying point for the struggle, Beatrice symbolizes anti-establishment. She would not be restrained by the dictates of culture not to be pragmatic enough to name Elewa's child, even when culture forbids. She debunks the myth of a male-dominated world, by performing the Naming Ceremony which is culturally seen as a man's duty. Her acceptance by Elewa's uncle and even the mother reluctantly, gives a glimpse of hope of an African society where gender would be a non-issue.

Defined by others as *"a quiet demure damsel"*, Beatrice at the beginning of the story could not define her feminist role. Achebe stresses this when he has Ikem say to Beatrice, *"I can't tell you what the new role for woman will be. I don't know .I should never have presumed to know. You have to tell us. We never asked you before"*. By the end of the story, Beatrice seems to have fulfilled Ikem's prophecy in defining her role in the struggle, by conducting the naming ceremony, a function hitherto seen as the prerogative of men.

Elewa
She is really a fine, fine girl

She is the girlfriend and fiancée of Ikem. Though of different ethnic group and even of social class from Ikem, yet they seem to share a deep sense of understanding.

Elewa is uneducated, yet, she is imbued with a self-awareness of her femininity. She frowns at the sexual exploitation of her body by Ikem. The irony is that, Ikem who is supposed to be more enlightened than Elewa has to take some lessons on proper treatment of a woman.

She possesses an aura and confidence, which does not give any room for inferiority complex. These attributes must have drawn the like of Ikem and even Beatrice to her who could not but ask, *"Why did she radiate this warmth and attraction and self-respect and confidence?...There was something in her that even her luckless draw could not remove"*. Her name which means, *"one who is imbued with beauty"* in Yoruba language confirms her personality.

Her courage in going through her bereavement with such stoic mien, presents her as a courageous young woman. She is however rewarded at the end of the novel with a child she bears for Ikem, who would symbolically represent a new Ikem.

Elewa is a study in courage in the face of various obstacles that could face a typical African lady. However, she does not allow any of these impediments to rob her of her essence as a woman. She surmounts all these to be counted among the heroines in the novel.

Emmanuel
Emmanuel went down and knelt beside him

He is the President of the Student Union of Bassa University. He emerges towards the end of the novel when Ikem addresses the students in his epoch making speech. Emmanuel is one of the fruits of Ikem's enlightenment seed on the need for the youths to be responsible enough to be able to be saddled with the leadership mantle of the nation.

Though inspired by Ikem, who does not live long enough to impart more into his life, yet he is able to quickly align himself with Chris who shows him practically what it means to be committed to the struggle to liberate the masses from the shackles of oppression of the ruling class. Unlike the older advocates, Emmanuel shows no lethargy in confronting the agents of oppression. The mobile police officers that are sent to arrest Emmanuel meet stiff opposition in frustrating the attempt.

The commitment of Emmanuel to the struggle is also shown when he abdicates his school work to join Chris in the *'underground train'*. Though he is on the wanted list of the government, yet going into hiding may not be the last option for him. *"Emmanuel was also a fugitive wanted by the police. But being of only middling importance in police estimation he was not given the VIP treatment of having his wait- and- take picture on television."*

Emmanuel takes his ingenuity and initiative further in the manner he ridicules and exposes the Press of Kangan, when he unsuspectingly places a story of Chris' escape to London. He is equally on the entourage of Chris as he makes his last journey to the *Great Northern Road* and even at the point of his gruesome murder.

Emmanuel, towards the end of the novel has consolidated himself as one of the pillars of the new community in Beatrice house. Though he seems not to have reached full maturity as a crusader, he is ever ready to learn from Beatrice who emerges as the leader of the new emerging front. He has come to share much with Beatrice and he gives her the last message of the *"Last Green Bottle"* which remains the only tangible memory Beatrice would live with for the rest of her life.

Young, vibrant, committed and daring, Emmanuel represents the future of Kangan where hope is rekindled.

THEMES

Feminism

Unlike in other works of Achebe, women play central roles. Women as a group or individuals, are central to themes of communal strength, relationality, solidarity and the transmission of cultural and spiritual values.

Women are relegated in a typical African society and Achebe sets out in his book to expose the evils against women. It is not surprising that his only surviving heroines are women in Elewa and Beatrice. What are the evils against women? Ikem could not fathom the meaning of responsibility, rather he would not see anything wrong in savouring Elewa sexually, but not ready to keep her company. Under the guise of a bad vehicle, Elewa is discarded like a used item. Beatrice suffers the same discrimination from childhood, where a typical African family values a male child above the female. Even at the height of her career, she could still not be accepted by a male-dominated society, where her rise is attributed to *'bottom power'*.

The universal basis for women degradation is further explored by the author who examines the issue from even the religious angle. He clinically examines the spectator role given to women as a way of men atoning for past abuse.

Though some of the men are trained in a society that respects women rights, they are still strongly influenced by their African orientation. Sam could not see why a woman should not be used to score political points, yet he could not find a woman worthy to be in his cabinet. The irony of some of the men's fight against societal ills is paradoxical. Ikem fights Sam because of his dictatorial tendencies, yet he could not fight his own chauvinistic attitude towards his girlfriend.

Achebe also emphasizes the importance of community, where women are presented as means of healing and as a source of strength for resistance. Beatrice plays the motherly role to Elewa during the time of her bereavement though she herself is mourning. She has to jettison her own pain to minister to the needs of Elewa. Thus personal relationships between women heighten a sense of solidarity that in itself is effective against oppression.

The war of sexes culminates at the Naming Ceremony of Elewa. Beatrice who becomes the beacon of the feminist struggle does what could be considered a taboo, when she names the baby in the absence of the male elder. Beatrice also becomes the rallying point for both male and female characters in the story who have one goal, which is to see the emergence of a better society.

Dictatorship

Although Kangan the mythical country in the novel is supposed to be independent, the influence of its former colonial masters (British) is still present. The departure of the colonialists leave a vacuum which is readily filled by a government dominated by tyrants and dictators who are equally as oppressive as the white colonists. Military dictatorship is often considered one of the banes of the African society and this is represented in Sam whose word is law. He rules by military fiat and he symbolizes the state.

Stratocracy engenders other allied vices such as alienation, class-consciousness and oppression. Like the former colonial masters, the ruling elite have alienated themselves from the masses they are supposed to represent and would rather send excuses: *"Tell them, if you like that I am on the telephone with the President of the United States of America or the Queen of England."* Beatrice makes the same observation on the desirability of the Presidential Retreat. Sam's programmes in the novel are motivated by self-perpetuation and preservation and never in the interest of the masses.

Despite the changes in the government, the essence of British attitude remains. The British lifestyle continues because the country's new leaders are products of the imposed European culture. Ikem, Beatrice, Sam and Chris are all educated in British schools and as such have modelled their lifestyles on their British orientation. These characters' affiliation with the white man brings them respect and maintains the wide gap established by the British between the government and the common people. The Attorney General confirms this *"You went to Lord Lugard College where half of your teachers were Englishmen. Do you know, the nearest white men I saw in my school were an Indian and two Pakistanis...?"*

The dilemma of Ikem for example is how he could still hold on to his British-oriented status quo and yet be able to maintain affinity with the masses he is supposed to lead. He gets more confused, because even the oppressed take delight in seeing their leaders exalted and cocooned in comfort, while they stand in *"blistering noontime heat awaiting the public executions..."*, Ikem could not fathom how the common man can bear to see shaded seats reserved for VIP's which remain vacant. However, by the end of the story, while Ikem and Chris are able to gain acceptance into the world of the masses, Sam remains aristocratic till the end.

The media are strictly controlled to serve the interest of the government. Information has to be censored because of the insecurity of the government not installed by democratic tenets. The government is so insecure that a mere solidarity visit by the Abazon people is seen as an invasion. This probably explains why Chris being the Information Commissioner and even Ikem are singled out for persecution in the story.

Dictatorship appears to have a negative influence on the psyche of the people. Capital punishment in whatever guise it would take would not change the people's attitude to crime. The impatience exercised by the drivers mirrors a tensed atmosphere in Kangan.

Ikem's lecture at the University of Bassa brings about the people's accommodation of what they term, "*democratic dictatorship*", which the speaker considers an aberration. Achebe appears to view democracy as individual responsibility. It is a consciousness where the people no matter their social class are mobilized to change the society. The author also castigates the practice of putting the state in the hand of a few oligarchs who may initially appear civil, but with time may bare their full fangs. Sam is a testimony.

The culmination of absolutism in the novel is the onslaught on the opposition where brutality, propaganda and wilful state power are used to subjugate the feeble opposition. Does the ending of the story indicate the defeat of dictatorship? Not exactly. Sam as symbol of totalitarianism is overthrown, but the structure of the system is still intact. The only glimpse of hope are found in the like of Emmanuel who is now imbued with a new consciousness to provide democratic leadership for Kangan.

Expression

Freedom of expression is one of the hallmarks of democracy, but in a stratocratic country like Kangan where military dictatorship is the order of the day, it is non-existent. Sam seems to understand this salient point. This explains why he is not disposed to the gathering of any form even by the Abazon people. He knows that such a gathering could engender words cum information which eventually translates to mobilization against any form of dictatorship. Sam himself who is a guru in the act of information manipulation also strategically puts his close friend, Chris, in charge of the Information Ministry, and most times, Sam feels that Chris does not manipulate information enough to suit the whims and caprices of the "*master*". Hear the master of the art speak: *'No television. Undue publicity .And before you know it, everybody will be staging goodwill rallies all over the place so as to appear on television...ask the Commissioner for Information to send a reporter across; and the Chief of Protocol to detail one of the State House Photographers to take your picture shaking hands with the leader of the delegation. But for God's sake Professor I want you to look at the man you are shaking hands with instead of the camera'.*

In a system where there is no freedom of speech, a character like Ikem takes it upon himself to be the people's mouthpiece. He does it with so much passion that he is able to make some changes in his environment. Though he may not have the raw power of Sam, yet he is as effective all the same. His editorial on the unsanitary state of the bus station and his attack on the capital punishment cause changes in these policies. The power of words as encapsulated in the essence of Ikem is appropriately described by the chief spokesman for the Abazons *"An animal whose name is famous does not always fill hunter's basket"* Though subtle, words are often more potent than raw power. The elder also adds enduring virtue to the power of words. *'The sounding of the battle –drum is important; the fierce waging of the war itself is important; and the story afterwards-each is important in its own way. I tell you there is not one of them we could do without .But if you ask me which of them takes the eagle feather I will say boldly: the story'...Recalling-is-Greatest... It is the story that outlives the sound of war-drums and the exploits of brave fighters. It is a story, not the others, that saves our progeny from blundering like blind beggars into the spikes of the cactus fence.*

In the end, when it is time for Sam to part ways with his two friends, it is because Ikem and Chris could not use their power of information to enhance the Life Presidency ambition of Sam. Ikem's slip of calling for the assassination of the President in his lecture at Bassa University is later used as an excuse to frame him up and subsequently get him murdered.

Reform

Anthills of the Savannah has every semblance of a social commentary as various knotty issues that bedevil the African continent are highlighted and the solutions where practicable are succinctly presented. Two issues that are often interplayed in the story are reform and revolution. Revolution may appear desirable to tackle the endemic and intractable problems of Africa, yet Achebe seems to have a better option in reforms and all these are cleverly woven into the characterization, the style, the setting and the themes of the novel.

Revolution seeks to proffer a drastic solution to problems and in most cases, it comes with violent takeover or change of social infrastructure and mechanisms. Sam when he overthrows might have been imbued with revolutionary zeal as most military dictators are, but with time when faced with the complexity and enormity of the problem, such a dictator may be too pride-filled to accept his mistakes and make the necessary corrections. In such situations, oppression, suppression and subjugation are often applied and instead of yielding positive results, things just worsen. This may be the situation with the capital punishment policy of the government of Kangan, where armed robbers are tied to stakes and are shot to the sadistic admiration of the spectators. Even in the sober ambiance that is supposed to characterize such a gathering, pickpockets still take delight in plying their trades. This situation clearly exemplifies the failure of a government policy borne out of force rather than understanding and diplomacy.

Achebe must have been influenced by the experience of postcolonial Africa characterized by military coups and civil wars, when using Ikem as his mouthpiece to advocate reform over revolution:

> *The sweeping, majestic vision of people rising like a tidal wave against their oppressors and transforming their world with theories and slogans into a new heaven and a new earth of brotherhood, justice, and freedom are at best illusions. The rising, conquering tide, yes; but the millennium afterwards, no! New oppressors will have been readying themselves secretly in the undertow long before the tidal wave really got going...reform may be a dirty word but it begins to look more and more like the most promising route to success in the real world...*

Achebe advocates psychological and spiritual solutions to the socio-political problems faced by the characters in colonial and post-colonial states. This kind of reform is supposed to be slow but enduring. It also called for individual responsibility rather than collective one. This reform does not trade blames nor is it reactive. According to Ikem:

> *But you cannot do that unless you first set about to purge yourselves, to clean up your act... You must develop the habit of scepticism...when you*

> have rid yourselves of these things, your potentiality for assisting this nation quadrupled.

Ironically, Ikem and Chris who advocate reform incidentally become the victim of senseless killings. The ending of the story however gives a glimpse of hope in the orientation of the new group that has gathered under the tutelage of Beatrice. They are united not by cultural, religious or economic interest, but the altruistic interest of their nation. They are awaiting the birth of a nation, where gender equality, fairness and love would reign.

WRITING TIPS

You and the Examiner
As in most writing endeavours, you are still writing with somebody in mind, but this time round, it is the faceless examiner, whose conditions ,whims, aspirations you must try to meet as the candidate writing the examination.

One point that must be clearly understood is that your purpose of reading a text is more than for pleasure. As such, the question of whether the text is boring or interesting does not arise .Whether you find the text interesting or not, it is your duty to develop interest in it in order to pass your examination. The examiner simply wants to know if you have the understanding of the text.

In view of this perspective, a text you are studying for your examination should be read more than once. The secret of reading is that the more you read, the more your confidence to answer any question on it. A text for the purpose of examination should be read at least three times.

What Style do I Adopt?
Every writer is unique. You have your own distinct style of writing and trying to write like the author is nothing short of being artificial. Avoid flowery and extravagant language with the wrong motive of impressing the examiner. Use appropriate vocabulary and style, which is simple, clear and concise.

Here are other tips to note:

- Avoid words whose meanings you are not so sure. Keep away from ambiguous words like *brilliant, super, excellent, nice* and even conjunctions like *however* and *moreover*. In addition, avoid slang words or casual phrases. These are words *like, terrific, fabulous, mind-blowing* etc

- Do not ask questions, except you are asking them rhetorically and they should be answered one way or the other.

- Watch the way you phrase your sentences such that they do not appear as if you want to force your argument on the examiner. In this vein, avoid extreme expressions such as, *"it is obvious that…"*, *"it can surely be seen that"*

- Personal pronouns such *I, we* should be avoided. Instead of writing *I think the author is trying to show the level of insecurity in the novel*, write, one *could claim that the author is trying to show the level of insecurity in the novel.*

- The tense to adopt in writing is present tense. Though practically the book was written many years ago, each time the book is read, the events in it come out fresh with new inspiration. Instead of writing *Elewa was the girlfriend and fiancée of Ikem* write, *Elewa is the girlfriend and fiancée of Ikem.*

How do I write my essay?

One erroneous belief is that the more you write, the higher your score would be. Such students write what they want to be asked instead of what has been asked. The escape route for such students is to reproduce a load of the entire story or a plot summary instead of answering precisely the question asked. So before you even start writing you must have asked and answered the question, *"would what I would write be wholly relevant to the question?"*

Writing is a process of presenting your argument, so you must sound convincing with all the relevant facts from the text. Do not just make a bogus claim without textual evidence. If for example, you wrote that Mad Medico a character in Chinua Achebe's <u>Anthills of the Savannah</u> is a racist, you should be able to draw empirical evidence from the text to back the claim. This is the why in a literary essay, there may not be a particular line of argument cum answer to an essay question. In most situations, as long as you can back up your claim with the necessary evidence and argument, you get the score that you deserve. A literary essay gives you the creative, imaginative freedom to maturely interpret a literary work. This explains why students who write pedestrian commentaries predictably get pedestrian marks!

The temptation in the examination hall is to write all you know about the question or topic. Practically the constraint of time does not make this feasible, so you must be imbued with such maturity that you can choose relevant facts from a deluge of information and then apply them to a specific area of the text and its content.

What structure should your essay take? It follows the usual pattern of an introduction, the body and the conclusion, but the most important ingredient that makes all these function is the constituent of the paragraph. A paragraph is a block of sentences that deals with just one topic or issue. Once you can understand this salient and simple truth, then you have mastered the most important soul of essay writing.

A paragraph starts with a topic or theme sentence. It is usually the opening sentence and it should sum up precisely what the paragraph is going to be about. This is followed by some lines to expatiate on the topic. Then comes a quotation or paraphrased illustration as evidence to prove your claim. The last and the most important step is to now give your own critical comment on the issue raised in the paragraph. If you like, you may add the concluding sentence. These are virtually the steps you follow to build the paragraphs that make up the entire essay.

There are other tips below:

The title of a published text is underlined. Eg _Anthills of the Savannah_ and that of an individual poem is placed in inverted commas- "Ode to a Nightingale". Do not forget to also write your title in full. _Things Fall_ is not the same as _Things Fall Apart_

Quotations are essential as your evidence in your essay, but caution should be exercised. Do not misquote or present a quotation wrongly. If you are not sure of the correct quotation, you can simply paraphrase. Do not also over quote especially if answering a context question. Try to somehow give a comment or two on the quotation. How do you go about having these quotations? The belief is that if you are so acquainted with the text, being able to quote accurately from it should not be a problem. However, if this is not the case, write down some relevant quotations and learn them by heart. Your teacher may be of help here.

To place your quotation, there is a format to follow. If the quotation is about three lines and above, you have to indent it, such that it stands out glaringly. On the other hand, if the quotation is about two lines or less, simply run it into the mainstream of your sentence. For example, _Though Ikem may be conscientious, yet "he could put a girl for taxi at midnight to go and jam with arm robbers in the road"_

Still on essay writing, it is imperative to plan. For an essay of one hour, the whole time is not meant for you to spend on writing the essay. At least five minutes should be spent on planning. Why do you need to plan? It simply helps you to see if you have enough points to tackle a question. Having arrived at the question to answer, understand the key terms in the question, as this would help you to unravel the question. Then get a rough paper and take your time to brainstorm, then organize your thoughts on the paper, allocating points to each paragraph. Think out the content of your introduction, the body and then your conclusion.

STUDY QUESTIONS ON
ANTHILLS OF THE SAVANNAH

1. How far could you claim that *Anthills of the Savannah* captures Achebe's ideals?

2. Critically analyse the symbolic representation of the **Sun** in the novel.

3. Explore the use of traditional narrative techniques to tell the story of contemporary relevance.

4. How does Achebe present women as the standard bearers of the struggle in the novel?

5. Discuss the appropriateness of the novel's title to its content.

6. *"An animal whose name is famous does not always fill a basket."* How does this portrayal depict Ikem?

7. Assess *Anthills of the Savannah* as a social commentary?

8. "*Anthills of the Savannah* is a story of clash between two conflicting social classes". Discuss.

9. "The novel is a story of power, of disillusionment of the responsibility of ordinary people for a change". Discuss.

10. Assess *Anthills of the Savannah* as a clash of the sexes.

11. "Like anthills surviving to tell the new grass of the Savannah about last year's bush fires". How does this statement reflect some themes in the novel?

12. *Anthills of the Savannah* is as much about expression as it is about alienation and reform." How far do you agree with this view?

SAMPLE ANSWERS

"Anthills of the Savannah is as much about expression as it is about alienation and reform." How far do you agree with this view?

Suggested notes for essay answer:

    (a) Expression and alienation are themes in the novel, but there are other themes like dictatorship, gender inequality, reform, etc.

    (b) Explore the theme of expression, which comprises of press freedom, the concept power of words as explained in the speech of the elder spokesperson of the Abazon.

    (c) The theme of alienation should be discussed-The gap between the ruler and the ruled, the rich and the poor.

    (d) The theme of reform is then looked at-look at reform as a tool of change as against revolution.

    (e) Look at other themes such as dictatorship, gender inequality, etc Allocate a paragraph or two to each of these points.

    (f) Conclusion-Comment on how these have explored the main subject matter of the novel.

How does Achebe present women as the torchbearers of the struggle in the novel?

    (a) Africa as a male-dominated society-Achebe giving prominence to the characterization of Elewa and Beatrice.

    (b) The role of Elewa, who despite being an illiterate, is still conscious of her right as a woman.

(c) The feminine perspective of the myth of Idemili and its relevance to female gender issues in Africa.

(d) Beatrice as a symbol of women struggle-Her modern perspective to issues-The abuse she suffers as a female child.

(e) Conclusion-Beatrice's triumph as the only surviving heroine in the midst of male contemporaries-her emergence as the leader of the new group.

SUGGESTIONS FOR FURTHER READING

Achebe, Chinua. *Things Fall Apart* .Ibadan: Heinemann Educational Books, 1958.
Achebe, Chinua. *No Longer at Ease* .Ibadan:Heinemann Educational Books,1960.
Achebe, Chinua. *Arrow of God* .Ibadan:Heinemann Educational Books,1964.
Achebe, Chinua. A *Man of the People*. Ibadan: Heinemann Educational Books, 1966.
Agetua, John (ed.). *Critics on Chinua Achebe, 1970-76* (Benin City, Nigeria: Bendel Newspapers Corp., 1977).
Egar, Emmanuel Edame. *The Rhetorical Implications of Chinua Achebe's 'Things Fall Apart'* (Lanham, Maryland: University Press of America, 2000). ISBN 0-7618-1721-2
Ekwe-Ekwe, Herbert. *African Literature in Defence of History: An Essay on Chinua Achebe* (Dakar: African Renaissance, 2001). ISBN 1-903625-10-6
Emenyonu, Ernest N. (ed.). *Emerging Perspectives on Chinua Achebe* (Trenton, New Jersey: Africa World Press, 2004). ISBN 0-86543-876-5 (v. 1), ISBN 0-86543-878-1 (v. 2)
Ezenwa-Ohaeto. *Chinua Achebe: A Biography* (Bloomington: Indiana University Press,   1997). ISBN 0-253-33342-3
Gikandi, Simon. *Reading Chinua Achebe: Language and Ideology in Fiction* (London : J. Currey, 1991). ISBN 0-85255-527-X
Innes, Catherine Lynette. *Chinua Achebe* (Cambridge, England; New York: Cambridge University Press, 1990).
Innes, C. L. and Bernth Lindfors (eds.). *Critical Perspectives on Chinua Achebe* (Washington: Three Continents Press, 1978.
Jaya Lakshmi, Rao V. *Culture and Anarchy in the Novels of Chinua Achebe* (Bareilly: Prakash Book Depot, 2003).
Killam, G. D. *The Writings of Chinua Achebe* (London: Heinemann Educational, 1977). ISBN 0-435-91665-3
Njoku, Benedict Chiaka. *The Four Novels of Chinua Achebe: A Critical Study* (New York: P. Lang, 1984). ISBN 0-8204-0154-4
Ogede, Ode. *Achebe and the Politics of Representation: Form Against Itself, From Colonial Conquest and Occupation to Post-Independence Disillusionment*

FURTHER READING

(Trenton, New Jersey: Africa World Press, 2001). ISBN 0-86543-774-2

Ojinmah, Umelo. *Chinua Achebe: New Perspectives* (Ibadan: Spectrum Books Limited, 1991). ISBN 978-2461-16-4

Okpewho, Isidore, (ed.). *Chinua Achebe's 'Things Fall Apart': A Casebook* (Oxford, England: Oxford University Press, 2003). ISBN 0-19-514763-4

Peterson, Kirsten Holst and Anna Rutherford (eds.). *Chinua Achebe: A Celebration* (Oxford, England: Dangeroo Press, 1991). ISBN 0-435-08060-1

Sallah, Tijan M. and Ngozi Okonjo-Iweala. *Chinua Achebe, Teacher of Light: A Biography* (Trenton, New Jersey: Africa World Press, 2003). ISBN 1-59221-031-7

Yankson, Kofi E. *Chinua Achebe's Novels: A Sociolinguistic Perspective* (Uruowulu-Obosi, Nigeria: Pacific Publishers, 1990). ISBN 978-2347-79-5

www.ingramcontent.com/pod-product-compliance
Ingram Content Group UK Ltd.
Pitfield, Milton Keynes, MK11 3LW, UK
UKHW041421180426
11947UKWH00007B/234